The Readiness Factor:

Preparing yourself for the Ultimate Relationship!

The Readiness Factor is published by:

Matters of the Heart, Inc.
3115 West 6th Street
Suite C-100
Lawrence, Kansas 66049

Copyright 1996 by Elaine Thompson, Ph.D. All rights reserved. No part of this book may be used or reproduced in any manner whatsoever without written permission. For information, please write to the address above.

Library of Congress CIP # 97-093418

Acknowledgments

****

I would like to thank God for the guidance and strength he offered me during this project.

I would also like to thank my parents: *To my mother*, Zepheree Stevens, who taught me the importance of having a strong belief in God and a never ending belief in myself and my abilities.

To My Father, Albert Stevens, who believed in education and worked hard to provide me with a good, solid education.

To all of the wonderful men and women who have come to me throughout the years for guidance, support and help. I hope I have offered sufficient help and assistance and I hope your life is a little easier because you trusted in my guidance.

Table of Contents

Introduction — Page 1

Chapter One
Timing is everything but readiness is the most important thing. — Page 6

Chapter Two
Everything must change, at it's own pace. — Page 21

Chapter Three
Esteem-building, in preparation for life's changes. — Page 42

Chapter Four
Self-preparation is the key to a positive, healthy relationship with another. — Page 58

Chapter Five
Now that I'm ready, where do I find quality people to go out with? — Page 78

Chapter Six
The Dating Game — Page 95

Chapter Seven
Committing to the relationship that feels right. — Page 108

Conclusion — Page 123
Bibliography — Page 126

Introduction

****

As a relationship consultant, founder of a matchmaking company, public speaker, and seminar leader, I truly understand how important healthy, fulfilling relationships are. I speak with individuals and couples each day about their relationship concerns and work very hard to help them understand and deal with their own particular issues.

I have had the privilege of working with some of the most wonderful individuals who wanted to be involved in a loving relationship with a self-sufficient, gentle human being. Some of them have come to me with a healthy sense of themselves, just wanting to add a person to their lives who would enhance what they already had inside of them.

Others have been bruised and battered by former lovers, parents and so-called friends, and they just want help in becoming better themselves so that they can bring a healthy, wholesome relationship into their lives.

Many of these people fail to realize that they already posses love within themselves. They just need to work toward exploring, finding and feeling that self-love. It is definitely the first step toward finding a true and special love with another.

The Readiness Factor is a practical guide to experiencing a healthy relationship with yourself and with others. It helps the reader understand that in order to have a satisfying and fulfilling relationship with another, you must have a healthy relationship with yourself.

It also helps the reader understand that change is very important in the process of preparing ourselves to be with another person.

Obviously, some changes are easier to make than others and when a person is ready to commit to making changes in their lives, they will. The changes can be personal or professional, but they will come at the right time. A person just needs to do what it takes to steer themselves toward change.

Many times that means working on becoming their best selves, and as positive changes happen inside of them, outside changes can begin to take form.

The Readiness Factor shows you how to successfully navigate a course through areas of your life so that you can create a healthier you through esteem-building. It shows you how you can emerge on the other side ready for the challenges of a positive, healthy relationship.

This book will help you understand that even though timing is everything, readiness is the most important thing when it comes to making decisions about relationships and other aspects of your life.

You will understand how important it is to take good care of your physical and mental health and how you can become your best self.

This will occur as a result of taking care of your physical needs, such as meditating, eating healthfully and exercising regularly.

You will also enjoy preparing yourself for an honest, healthy relationship with another. You will learn how and where to meet others, and how to tell whether or not to move forward into a relationship once you have met someone special.

You will learn which topics are crucial for discussion before entering into a committed relationship and/or marriage and you will learn how to deal with differences as far as these topics go.

Once in a marriage, you will learn several ways to keep the sparks going in the relationship and how to keep love alive.

My view on love is that it is the greatest emotion one can feel and there are so many of us who search a lifetime for the love that we feel we should possess. Others can have a great and wonderful love within their grasp and simply not allow the love to flourish because of unreadiness and unsteadiness.

Obviously, being ready to accept true love in it's purest and most innocent form is available to many of us, so we need to "ready" ourselves for that true love. For, if we are not prepared, love can slip away and be gone very quickly.

Read this book and understand the power of readiness and preparation for a true and honest love. It is indeed empowering when we take the time to work on making ourselves the very best that we can be. That's what life and love are all about; continuous learning, experiencing and growing.

Remember, self-love is absolutely the greatest and first love we must have. When we truly love ourselves, and prepare ourselves for the love of another, then and only then, will we be ready, willing and able to enjoy all of the sincere pleasures that having the love of another can bring.

Chapter One

Timing is everything but readiness is the most important thing.

****

This is a book about readiness and what it takes to prepare yourself for a wholesome, healthy relationship.

You see, in the grand scheme of things, it really doesn't matter if you are in the right place at the right time and if you just happen to meet the right person at the right time. If you are not "ready" for a relationship, most of the time, it will not work.

It does not matter what the other person says, does or even feels, if you are not "ready", timing will not mean anything.

Let me give you an example. When Tracie met Kevin in 1993, she was so excited. He was handsome, romantic, generous and easy to talk to. They spent the entire evening talking about everything under the sun and she discovered that they had a lot in common. When the night was over, she called two of her best girlfriends and said to each of them; "I was just in the right place at the right time. I could not believe it because I almost didn't go out tonight. Most of all, I just broke up with Josh so this was perfect timing."

Both of her girlfriends were delighted for her and she kept them up with all of the adventures because she and Kevin saw each other every day for a week. However, even though they were very compatible and really enjoyed each other, Tracie had not taken the proper time to grieve through her previous relationship and she brought all of that emotional turmoil to the new friendship with Kevin.

Eventually, things got uncomfortable because Tracie spoke of Josh often and in a negative way because she was still hurt and in need of a cooling out period to properly grieve the previous relationship.

Kevin stopped calling Tracie as much because he felt uncomfortable listening to her negative stories about her ex. Eventually, he told her that he would not see her anymore because of his discomfort.

Tracie felt hurt and felt that Kevin was just as bad as all the other guys and that he never gave the relationship a chance. Of course this was a double dose of pain because she had not dealt with the other loss.

As you can see, Kevin may have been a great match for her but Tracie was not "ready" for Kevin and the type of relationship he had to offer her. She did not see that she had to take the time to work through the ending of the first relationship before she could enter into a new one.

This particular situation is a tough one because when we are feeling wounded, as Tracie was feeling, we want to go out immediately and find comfort to cover up some of the suffering. That's why she went out immediately after the end of the relationship with Josh. She wanted to find a "replacement", but she needed to work through the loss instead.

This is just one example of "readiness". There are so many situations that fit this. For instance, it does not matter what the situation is, if one person is not ready for the same thing as the other person, the relationship will have to go through some turmoil and troubled times.

Also, if two people meet and feel that they are on the same page, quite often, over time, one of them will change or grow into another "readiness stage" while the other person is still quite content where he or she is. Let me tell you about a couple I am currently working with.

Joyce and Howard met four years ago and there was a lot of chemistry. At the time they met, Joyce had a lovely home of her own which she shared with her teenage daughter. Joyce had been divorced for 13 years and dated a little but not a lot. Howard had been divorced for many years also and lived alone in his own home. When they met, they began to spend a lot of time together and soon they were spending all their weekends together and taking great trips during the summer months. They traveled during the summer because Joyce was a teacher and had the summers off. Howard owned his own business and could take off whenever they wanted to go away. They were both very happy and content with the relationship. You see, at the onset of the relationship, they each made it very clear that they did not want to be married at all.

Things were going well and Joyce's daughter moved to Chicago to live with her fiancée' so Joyce and Howard mutually decided to sell Joyce's house so that she could move in with Howard. Joyce was not particularly fond of Howard's furniture so they bought some new pieces and spruced things up a bit so Joyce could feel more at home. This helped a little but Joyce began to feel unsettled and could not figure out why. That's when they came to see me. After a few sessions, we figured out that somewhere between selling her home and moving in with Howard, she decided that she wanted more of a commitment and that she was ready to work toward marriage.

She was really shocked that she began to feel like this because she had gone for four years and not felt that she needed marriage. She had been totally content and felt quite free and good about the way things were going.

When she confessed her feelings to Howard, he made it perfectly clear that he did not want to be married and that he was fine with things the way they were. He confessed that he was afraid of marriage again because his wife had abandoned him after 12 years of marriage. He never wanted to experience that again.

It was very clear to me that the relationship was in jeopardy. Joyce and Howard were very much in love but while Joyce's needs had changed, Howard was satisfied with things as they were. He was not ready to change and was willing to risk the relationship at this point because his fears and concerns were bigger than his relationship with Joyce.

It is very obvious that Howard is not ready to move toward marriage again. He is afraid that he will experience the same catastrophe as he did with his first marriage and he is shielding himself from that because he does not want to repeat the pain and experience. In other words, he has a serious fear of failure.

Many of us are guilty of this. We refuse to take on a project or make a decision for fear that we will fail, out lives will be miserable and people will see us as failures. Successful people know, however, that it is often necessary to fail before you can succeed.

But for many people, just the possibility of failure is enough to keep them from trying. Obviously, this is the case with Howard. His fear of failure is so strong that he cannot see past it and cannot commit to trying again, even though the first marriage ended many years ago.

As I did some probing into Howard's childhood, I discovered that when he made a mistake or failed to do a task to his father's satisfaction, he was punished. When this happened, Howard felt that his father did not love him and consequently, Howard linked failure to the loss of love.

Many parents punish their children for failing because they feel that it will encourage them to do better but, often, this kind of parenting teaches children that the price for failure is loss of love. None of us can afford to pay that price, so for those who believe that failure will cost them love, even thinking of a change that might end in failure is too big of a risk. For Howard, it's a double whammy because if his fear of failure keeps him from marrying Joyce he loses her love and if he marries her and the marriage fails, he loses the love of his father, or in his mind he does. So, you see, this is mentally challenging for Howard.

One thing that is very important in helping Howard is to help him deal with his apparent fear of failure.

We have been acculturated to think that failure is bad and always has negative consequences. This is not true. Some of my personal failures have been some of my best learning experiences and I became much better as a result of experiencing them.

Howard needs to ask himself; "what's the worst that could happen if this marriage fails?" If he can get to a point where he can accept the possibility that although the relationship is not guaranteed to work, the two of them have a solid chance, maybe he can work toward a commitment to marriage. However, if things do not work out, how will he deal with it and make it a learning experience once the grieving is over?

One thing's for sure. He has been with Joyce for four years and out of that four, they have lived together for one year so they have a great foundation. They are both in their forties so they are not kids anymore and maybe this will make a difference. Whatever happens, Howard has his work cut out for him and if he is willing to work toward change, he can do it at his own pace and feel good about it. Howard will be ready for change when, no matter what happens, he can survive the consequences that the change will bring, whether positive or negative.

As for Joyce, what should she do in the meantime?

Joyce has made it very clear that she wants a commitment of marriage from Howard and that if he cannot at least move in that direction, she will move out of his house and get her own place again. She has no idea when or if she can make this move and she is quite hesitant because of her love for him. However, it is quite clear to her that she needs some sort of movement in the relationship and she needs to set goals and have direction.

You see, Joyce is more of a risk-taker than Howard but she still is not a high risk taker and there has always been comfort in having Howard there. She has her fears also but they are not fears of committing to marriage. Her fears are a little different.

14

I encouraged Joyce to continue to live her life fully and to continue to grow and develop as an individual. I encouraged her to continue to look at the relationship with openness and to explain and make clear to Howard at all times what she needed and wanted. I explained to her that if she makes changes in herself that are comfortable, (moving out, meeting new people, etc.), she will increase her esteem and feel good about who she is and what she wants.

I explained to her that she should not feel bad about who she is and what she wants and that it is perfectly normal to ask for a commitment at this point, but I also explained to her that she knew at the onset of the relationship that Howard would not consent to marriage.

I explained to her that just because she changed, she should be honest with herself and continue to be in touch with her feelings. She has a right to change and she should continue growing and feeling good about her changes.

During our most recent session, Joyce told me that she had been looking at houses and that she was definitely moving out. Howard seemed fine with her decision and has decided that he still is not ready for marriage. He made it very clear, however, that he still loves Joyce very much and has no desire to stop seeing her or end the relationship. Joyce seemed to concur and they plan to continue to date.

It will be interesting to see where this relationship goes in the future. They each have some soul searching to do and I will do my best to help them individually and as a couple.

So, as you can see, timing *is* everything but readiness is the most important thing when it comes to relationships. If the two people involved in the relationship are not at the same readiness level at the same time, they will have some struggles. At times, these relationships do work out but they definitely require work.

That's why it is very important to do what it takes to prepare yourself for the right relationship. Also, take enough time to be sure that your potential partner is at a readiness level comparable to yours.

In some cases, such as Joyce and Howard, couples can start out at the same readiness level and then grow apart through the years. This is reality and even though these are hard situations to deal with, many times with hard work, love and commitment to work through the process, couples can emerge on the other side, stronger and more in love than ever.

However, in some cases, two people can meet, feel really good about each other, spend a few days, weeks or even months together and feel great excitement about finally finding "the one." Then, all of a sudden, without warning, one of them will disappear, stop calling or totally ignore the other person. This leaves that person feeling rejected, hurt, confused and asking questions such as, "what did I do or say to drive the person away?"

Actually, there may not have been anything you did or said. The person could have simply thought they were ready for the type of relationship the two of you had and suddenly realized that they definitely were not ready. They fled because of their own fear. This is a form of commitment phobia that we will discuss later in the book.

Undoubtedly, the obvious question is, why did the person just leave without talking to me about his or her feelings? The answer to this is that it is far

17

easier to ignore and disappear than it is to come forward. That takes true courage and requires the person to be a mature woman or man and many people who have problems with readiness and commitment are not at that level of maturity.

Consequently, the best advice concerning new beginnings is, take your time and get to know the person. Tune in to what the person is doing and saying and slowly get to know who the person truly is. This does not guarantee that the person will stay around but if he or she doesn't, at least you have not invested a large chunk of your heart into something that fizzled very quickly and without warning.

In conclusion, remember these readiness rules:

1. Always take time to heal following a break up. No matter how tempted you are, do not get involved with a new person before you have resolved your feelings for a previous relationship that did not work.

2. If you and your partner are not at the same readiness level at the onset and you want a committed relationship, do not hang around hoping he or she will change. Look for someone who is at your particular

level of readiness and work toward building with that person.

3. Beware of the person who tells you they are looking for a commitment, only to get you to spend time with them. While these people are hard to spot, if you take your time getting to know the person and allow your good instincts and gut feelings to lead you, you will be able to tell whether or not the person is genuine most of the time. However, we all can become victims of these "sweet talkers" so if you do, take the experience with you on your next journey and use your experience to better help you in the future. Do not beat up on yourself because these "sweet talkers" are masters at what they do and they can fool just about anyone.

4. Do not allow the "stars in your eyes" to blind you to what is real. Take a close look at what your potential partner is saying but tune in to what he or she is doing. Talk is easy for some people and they will figure out what you need to hear and fill you up with it. Watch what the person does, more so than what he or she says and take your time and get to know

the person better before you commit your heart totally.

5. Most of all, have fun looking for a person at your same readiness level. Let it flow, be natural and give it time.

Chapter Two

Everything must change, at it's own pace.

****

In order to become "ready" for the ultimate relationship, we often find the need to make changes in our lives. However, as we know, change can be frightening and because of this, we all avoid change in certain situations. We may know exactly what we want to happen when we make a desired change, but no one can precisely predict the outcome of that change before it is made.

We can't forecast the result of the change we want to make, but we can imagine it, and when we think about the probable outcome of such a change, most of us envision the worst-case scenario. Often we believe that the worst thing that can happen will happen and, real or imagined, this expectation has the power to keep us from changing.

One thing we can do is ask ourselves, "What will happen if I make this change?" Make a list of the possibilities, positive and negative, and look at the lists. Once you do this exercise, you will be able to focus on whether or not the positive points outweigh the negative points. You will then be able to make a decision once you have weighed all of the consequences, good and bad. Consequently, until you know that no matter what happens you can handle it, survive the experience and go on with your life, you probably will not be able to make a change.

We are often guilty of shielding ourselves from potential pain and suffering. We don't want to venture out because we feel that we could be hurt, physically or mentally and it is far easier to stay where we are. At least we know what this feels like and we don't have to risk the potential of any pain and suffering.

Because of this, many people spend their entire lives securely on the solid ground of the known. Sometimes we wonder what it would be like to cross over to the other side but we won't take that leap.

Some of us will move toward a different situation, then move back to the security of what is familiar.

It is so clear when you see people who stay in dead-end jobs and negative, unfulfilling relationships. They prefer to accept a familiar pain than risk something unfamiliar that they see to be far worse than what they have now. They say things like, "at least I have a pay check every two weeks, even though I will never be promoted", or "well, he *is* a good provider, even though we don't talk much and I don't see him on weekend nights."

For these people, life may be unpleasant or even painful, but it is a familiar discomfort or pain. They feel that at least life will not expose them to any unfamiliar pain that they do not know how to deal with.

When you try something for the first time, you generally cannot predict what will happen. You may be expected to do things you don't know how to do; you may have to learn a new skill; you may be surprised, caught off guard, or even seen as incompetent.

There can be real dangers involved when the change is something like learning to ski, sky dive or fly a plane.

Changing careers, moving to another state, or going back to school can hold unknown surprises also, along with first dates, new marriages and many other changes that we undertake.

No matter how well you prepare or how hard you work, most of the time, you cannot guarantee the outcome of the risk you want to take. This is a fact that some people find hard to accept. They spend all of their time and energy trying to produce a desirable result and this may or may not happen. No change comes with a guarantee. There will be changes in our lives that will produce negative results, hurt feelings and sadness but this is all part of life and growth.

All in all, until you feel that you can survive the pain of whatever is going on, not risking is the easiest choice you can make. You have to know that you can survive the worst before you can feel good about taking the risk.

Often in our lives we want to do certain things that we have never done before. However, we are so afraid and because of our fear, we try to make sure that everything is absolutely perfect before we take that leap.

For instance, we might have the perfect partner for ourselves, but we will not propose marriage until we have enough money saved or until we can buy a great house, etc. Consequently, what often happens is that while we are "getting it all together", things change and we might miss out on that person.

If you actually do decide to take a risk and do something uncomfortable to you, go ahead and try. If you are successful and the change that you make works out, wonderful. However, if you have thought about it and worked on the possibilities and you still cannot make the change, it's all right. It just means that you are not ready to make the change. That's fine. Just continue to work on yourself and continue to work toward small, positive changes in your life. You'll be surprised to see that when you are truly ready to make a change in your life, you will do just that and you will be much stronger and better able to deal with all of the consequences, positive and/or negative.

Many times, we are guilty of basing our expectations of what will happen to us on what has already happened in our past. This is quite normal and is a human reaction.

For instance, if we showed affection to someone we loved in the past and that person rejected us, we are more likely to shy away from showing affection in the future. This is especially true if our parents rejected our affections. It is more difficult to show love as an adult.

On the other hand, if our past experiences were pleasant and positive, we expect to have positive experiences and we move forward with greater ease and take risks more easily.

Some of the most powerful past experiences are those which we received negative reactions for simply being ourselves. For instance, if we were naturally smart, shy, sensitive or physically beautiful, people may have rejected us because of their own insecurities. This rejection could have caused us to feel that we needed to change in order to fit in with our peers.

For instance Gail was strikingly beautiful from the time she was a tiny baby. Everyone spoke of her beauty and, many times, she was stared at when she went out. When she became a teenager, the boys in school were intimidated by her and the girls were very jealous and did not want her around. Gail felt like an outcast and she was very bothered by the reactions that she received from her peers. She decided that she had to make some changes so that she could be liked. She decided that maybe if she were loud and funny, people would like her so she developed a new personality and it actually did help her and she did obtain a few friends. However, she was not being herself and this was not comfortable for very long. She then decided that she had to keep up this facade but in order to do it, she needed to drink so that she could pretend. She began to drink a little and this helped but when the boys realized that she drank, they began to take advantage of her and she became promiscuous. This was not good for her reputation which then attracted other types of friends and eventually, in the midst of self-destruction, she wound up in rehabilitation and counseling. Anyway, this was the best thing that could have happened to her and it probably saved her life. Now, she has to deal with all the issues that led her there in the first place.

Gail will have to take a long, hard look at who she really is and work toward accepting herself as she is and dealing with rejection from others who might be intimidated by her. She will need to change her perceptions of needing to fit in and search out genuine people who will accept her just as she is. This change is necessary for her to have a fulfilling life and when she is ready, she will make the necessary mental changes and work toward self-satisfaction.

There are several reasons why people resist change. However, one of the biggest reasons is that people feel they are safe as long as they remain as they are. Most people do not like to go beyond their comfort zone. Some feel that they have reached the limit of how far they can go and they no longer want the stress and anxiety of adjusting their present situation. They do not want to imagine what they can be, because they are not ready to make that shift. Consequently, they prefer to stay with the familiar and within their own zone of comfort.

Here are some suggestions for personal empowerment:

*Go beyond your comfort zone on a regular basis. Encourage yourself to take risks, starting with small ones and working your way up to the larger ones. Talk to yourself and say positive things. Tell yourself that you can accomplish tasks that you have put off because of discomfort, then perform the task. If you succeed, praise yourself and move on to the next adventure. If you extend yourself and the result is negative, try again. Do not allow yourself to be defeated.

*Think of yourself as a person who has everything you need to be all that you can be. Many of us feel that we are missing some element, therefore, we do not have what we need to obtain what we want. When we begin to focus inward and think of ourselves as being fully equipped to tackle any adventure, we will make more of an effort.

*Focus on the fact that all of your actions are controlled by your mind. In other words, all actions are in direct response to a powerful mental stimulus. Get to know and understand this and use it to your advantage. It will supply you with the power you need to make changes in your life.

*Practice the art of positive thinking. This is one of the most important things you can do for yourself. It is also one of the most difficult because we are faced with negativity every day. We must fight to remain positive. Remember, negativity stunts our growth and prohibits us from moving forward.

*Become less judgmental. When you look at other people's lives, instead of judging them, focus on what has brought them to the place they are in, not necessarily where they are or what they are doing. Try to be more empathetic and less judgmental.

*Learn to take better care of your physical and mental health. Be sure to incorporate quiet, peaceful time into your schedule. Make time to choose healthy foods and to exercise more.

*Be patient with yourself. The process of change is a difficult one and requires time and patience. Remind yourself of what a wonderful human being you are and of how you will always be a work in progress, never finished but continuously getting better. When you do things that you deem unsatisfactory, forgive yourself. Do not beat up on yourself unmercifully. This is negative and never helps. Evaluate what you did, think of what you could have done differently and work toward a positive change. Never remain in a negative place. It is self-defeating. The beauty of treating yourself well is that the better you treat yourself, the better you will treat others and the better others will treat you.

Most of all, remember that when you are in a state of readiness, you will be mentally aware that you can survive any changes that may come your way.

One thing to remember as you are making changes is that some changes are harder to make than others and often, we are able to make certain changes fairly easily. However, there are certain changes that are very difficult and quite painful. For instance, it might be less difficult for a wife to leave an abusive husband if there are no children involved, but it might be close to impossible for a wife to leave if there are children involved and she is unemployed. She could still make a transition, but it would be very difficult and involve careful planning and timing.

Making difficult changes is something that many of us choose to avoid because we have been acculturated to believe that major changes which may negatively effect others is wrong. It can create pain and sadness which some feel can be avoided.

How often have you decided to make a difficult change and when you share your mission with a friend or family member, you get resistance? They often say things like. "What's the matter with you? Can't you just leave well enough alone?" or "How could you just leave your wife? Remember the vows you took?" They feel that it is better to remain in a familiar situation no matter how painful it is.

However, if you have gotten to a point in your life where your pain has become unbearable and you are ready to find comfort and contentment again, you must take action. I repeat, *you must take action.* There is a good, solid reason you are feeling the way you are and you must act on this right away. Do not allow others to make you feel guilty about your decisions. This could keep you stuck in an unhealthy place. Even if your decisions are unpopular with your loved ones, they are the right decisions for you.

This is very difficult because you feel that if you make certain changes, you will lose the love or respect of others who are important to you. Even though this is understandable, it is only when you are able to love yourself most of all and not depend on the approval or acceptance of others that you will be able to make positive changes in your life. You must accept the fact that your decision might not be the most popular one with others, but it is the best one for you.

When you get to the point where your pain is more important than being popular or maintaining so-called friendships, you are well on your way because your true friends will stick by you no matter what. Always remember that. You are the one who has to live with you, not anyone else. You are the one who has to realize that often a decision for movement can save your life, so be strong, take the time to make a solid plan and move toward making the necessary changes to improve your life.

As you make these changes, some people will feel as though you have lost it or that you are "breaking down." People will view this as negative because we have been led to believe that breaking down, losing it or falling apart are negative, inappropriate actions and people try to avoid these actions at all costs. This is so ironic because when you remain in a place that has become uncomfortable or that is no longer working for you, eventually, you *will* lose it because you have tried to remain with the familiar and it has become unhealthy.

Breaking down is a normal reaction to pain, fear and sadness and there is absolutely nothing wrong with an occasional breakdown. Many times we need to break down in order to get up and make changes in our lives. Sometimes, breaking down is the only way our bodies know how to let us know that we are miserable and that the charade has gone on long enough and it is time for movement and for changes to take place.

The good news is that you do not have to make these difficult changes alone. Find a therapist, support group, anonymous program, or peer group with which to discuss this. Nonjudgmental, supportive friends and family members are key to help you through this also.

Most important, you need to know that even if you feel that you are losing it, you are perfectly normal. You are just in a situation that needs attention, time and change in order for you to get through. Also, understand that what is happening to you is good, not bad and that this is the way people make changes that will make their lives better. Know that it will not last forever, but that it is a necessary and important step in the process of healing and when this is over, you will be much healthier and happier than before.

Remember, you must love yourself enough to know when you are in a situation that is non-productive and headed for destruction. When your entire being is giving you clues that there is something you need to change, go inward and listen. Meditate, get quiet and allow yourself to feel whatever your body is trying to help you feel.

As you go inward, remember that you might have to give up the dream that someone else can fill up the empty place inside you and make you feel whole and safe. First of all, it is entirely too much pressure to put on another person and the burden for them will eventually cause separation. Consequently, *you* must be the source of your security. Your safety depends on your loving yourself, because as long as you imagine that your safety depends on someone else's continuing love, you can't afford to risk losing it or them. That keeps you stuck in an unhealthy place with no possible way out under any circumstances. That is stifling, unproductive, difficult and creates an illusion.

Your need to feel safe, however, is not an illusion. We all need to feel safe; that is the foundation on which we build our lives. However, no matter how good it feels in the short run, the love or approval of another is not a true foundation. You can and must be the one who loves you. You can and must be the master builder of your own foundation. But how?

Growing up requires each of us to pass through various developmental stages. At each stage certain conditions must be present if we are to successfully complete our developmental tasks. For example, you will learn to trust only if, when you're dependent and helpless, your environment is safe and secure. You learn independence only if, when you're ready to chance separation, your parents are able to let you go. If you reach a developmental stage and the conditions aren't right, a part of you doesn't develop, you don't learn to trust or be independent. A part of you remains the age it was when your development was interrupted. This is what is meant by the "inner child."

If, as a child, you didn't learn to trust or to be independent, there will be behaviors that, as an adult, you will have difficulty accomplishing; anything that requires trust or independence. Fortunately, that "child" still lives inside of you, and it's still possible to correct the error of your childhood, to create the conditions under which the developmental stage can be completed and to have the happy life as an adult that you should have had as a child.

Creating the conditions under which a part of yourself can move through a missed developmental stage may require you to treat yourself in exactly the opposite way that your family treated you. You may have to love and accept yourself unconditionally, and this may be the opposite of what you believe you deserve. You may not get much support from your family or friends, consequently, the work of becoming the one who loves you could be quite difficult. However, if you're ready to accept the challenge of becoming the one who loves you, there are many books and articles written about the art of self-love, so you will not have trouble getting the help you need.

Self-discovery however, is a lifetime job. Find the courage you need to explore some of your childhood messages and evaluate how they have affected your life and personality in general. You will realize how your past has made you the individual you are today. Then, and only then, can you seriously begin to replace those messages and actions with new ones.

Let me give you an example. Crystal was the youngest of six children and by the time she became a teenager, her parents had worked their way to a nice, comfortable living. Because she was in high school, she needed money to take care of all of her high school expenses. Her parents had not allowed her to begin working at that point so she had to depend on them for money. This had been fine up to this point because she had always gone to her mother for money but her mother had begun to tell her that she had to ask her father for any money she needed. This was quite difficult for Crystal because whenever anyone asked her father for money, he would frown, ask a million questions, and generally make the person feel uncomfortable. Because of this, Crystal would go without what she needed until she became desperate. Then, she would carefully plan the activity. She had to figure out the best day of the week, the best time of day and the circumstances. Generally, this would be on Sunday, during a baseball game on TV. and during the right commercial. She would stand at the door of the room where he was and wait for the proper time, then, terrified, she would make her entrance, ask the question and with sweaty palms, await the outcome.

Needless to say, she could not continue to do this so she eventually convinced her mother to let her work part-time.

The good news is that she developed a sense of independence and learned at an early age how to get her needs met on her own. The unpleasant news, however, is that she feels that she has to make it in the world without ever asking anyone for anything. Because of this she has become very isolated as an adult and still has that feeling whenever she has to ask anyone for even the slightest favor. Her independence has become unhealthy and is affecting her life in a negative way. Because of this, she needs help in working through the teenage experience so that she can live a more normal life.

I explained to her that we all need someone at some point in our lives and that she will never live a wholesome, free life until she works through this.

So, all in all, everything must change, at it's own pace. We just need to be able to see and understand when something is affecting our life in a negative way and when we need to make these changes. If our needs are not being met and our lives are not what we want them to be, we need to work toward making changes. Maybe it will take weeks, months or even years. The most important part is that we are working toward changes that will make our lives better, more complete and healthier.

The bottom line is that everything must change. That is one guarantee in life. Change is inevitable and whether you are changing the hard way or the easy way, change will occur when you are physically and mentally ready for it to occur. If you have discovered something in your life that needs changing, work toward that change. Take small steps and move forward. It's OK to take tiny steps toward your goal. At least you are moving in the right direction and once the change occurs, it will be worth all the time, effort and energy you have put forward and you will feel a wonderfully special sense of accomplishment.

Chapter Three

Esteem-building, in preparation for life's changes

****

In order to make necessary changes in our lives, we must have healthy, fulfilling relationships with ourselves. This is very important for us to understand. We have to be totally honest with ourselves and take some time to figure out important aspects of who we are. This includes self-examination and a sincere willingness to work toward greater self-esteem.

I understand that the term self-esteem has been steadily used in the self-help market today and I also understand that we are probably tired of hearing it.

It seems as though when people tell us that we need to build our self-esteem, they are saying that we are not good and whole as we are. Many of us resent this because we know in our hearts that we are quite good and that we have many wonderful qualities. We like ourselves as we are so why do these so-called "experts" have to keep telling us that we are not good enough just as we are?

When we feel that someone is telling us that we are not good enough, we resist their suggestions, help and assistance because we feel that if we give in to their suggestions, we are indeed admitting that we are not good. Then, of course, we feel bad about who we are because the so-called "expert" told us that we need to work on ourselves.

This can cause resistance and keep us from what really is a life-long process. In other words, when we realize that working on ourselves does not mean working on ourselves until we are "fixed", or until we feel better, it means that we will always work toward becoming better. I think it is easier to accept and deal with if we put it in that context.

The bottom line is, <u>esteem-building is a life-long process.</u> We will need to work on ourselves for the rest of our lives. Once we feel good about one aspect, we need to move on to the next aspect, and so on. This does not mean that we will spend all of our time working on ourselves. It just means that in order to grow, we have to be aware of our need to continuously feed our bodies with knowledge and an understanding of ourselves and our changing needs.

Our world changes so often and so do we. We age, we mature and our life circumstances change. We need to be aware of these changes and nurture ourselves accordingly with new and better information.

In order to have a positive view of ourselves, we *must* have a healthy and positive self-esteem. It will help us succeed in life and understand ourselves better. It will help us abide by our own standards instead of someone else's. It will also decrease our feelings of inadequacy and self-doubt.

We deserve happiness and in order to know and believe this, we have to feel good about ourselves and have a positive vision of ourselves.

Self-esteem is a combination of self-confidence and self-respect. It is the art of knowing that you are a capable and valuable human being. It is what you think of yourself, not what others think of you.

There are a number of reasons why we must work on increasing our self-esteem. People with a high level of esteem are:

*More likely to form positive, healthy relationships
*More in touch with their emotional and spiritual sides
*More tolerant and respectful of themselves and others
*More well-rounded in the basic aspects of their lives.

When we feel good about ourselves, we respect ourselves and when we respect ourselves, we respect others. We treat ourselves well and we treat others well. We do not try to put others down in order to make ourselves feel better or more superior.

Remember, the things that are happening to us on the outside are a reflection of what is going on inside of us. Some people tend to search for self-confidence and self-respect outside of themselves instead of looking within. This does not work and leads to disappointment and confusion.

For example, Anna is a beautiful young woman in her twenties. She is well-educated, beautiful and would be considered by others to "have it all." She searches for love and respect from superstars, such as athletes and entertainers. She feels that if she is dating people with high recognition, she will feel important because people will respect the fact that she is able to be with these famous people. However, this does not work very well for Anna because she finds that these types of men are very much in demand and for her they are "here today and gone tomorrow", which makes her feel even worse about herself. She then finds another athlete or entertainer and the pattern repeats itself over and over but she still does not see that her search for importance is not in the men she dates. It is within her. She is obviously doing the same thing over and over expecting different results and she will never acquire a high level of self-esteem if she continues to look outside herself.

In order to raise our self-esteem, increase our level of self-confidence and self-respect, we need to exist in the "here and now." We need to be aware of what we are doing and how we are acting at all times. We need to understand how important it is to live in the present moment, being conscious and aware of what we are feeling at all times and living this way. This helps us feel better about ourselves because it is very honest and creates a firm foundation.

We must make a commitment to be aware of how we are feeling in our inner world and how we are behaving in our outer world. This does not mean that we will like and approve of everything we see but that we recognize that which is real is real. Wishing and hoping things were different does not change what is really real. Only we have the ability to change our world and make it better if we choose to. Consequently, in order to make positive changes, we must first see things for what they really are.

We need to be aware of the child in us as well as the adult in us. It is very important that we recognize the child in us and nurture and respect that part of ourselves. Many times our fears and insecurities come from the child within us. This can be scary to deal with and many of us avoid these scary feelings and substitute them with more pleasurable ones.

Let me tell you about a client I have been working with. His name is Alan. Alan has many fears which stem from a childhood heavily laden with fears which his parents perpetuated. However, his main fear that we are dealing with at this time is his fear of flying.

You see, Alan has missed out on a huge part of his life because he hates to fly and will do almost anything he can to avoid it. When he knows he has to fly, he gets so nervous and afraid, his entire metabolism changes. He has butterflies, cannot eat, has restless nights and is quite irritable.

His doctor prescribed tranquilizers for him and he will use them if he is forced to fly but he avoids flying like the plague.

He is afraid now because his career is changing and he will have to fly or miss professional opportunities which he has worked very hard to obtain. This is why he asked me to help him with this fear.

It is very obvious that he needs to find a way to conquer, or at least deal with this fear in order to advance in his career. I explained to him that he might not actually get over his fear but maybe we can think of some ways for him to get through the experience safely and securely without as much tension.

Some suggestions were that, until he felt comfortable, he might want to use the medication prescribed by the doctor for a couple of flights, then he might want to have a glass of wine instead so that he will not continue to depend on the medication. Hopefully, eventually, he will not even need a glass of wine.

I also suggested that he take a cassette player and listen to very soothing music during the flight with his eyes closed and some deep, calm breathing.

I recommended some reading materials and an actual "fear of flying" course offered by a pilot.

Our fears, insecurities and dependencies are very real and are part of our child within. Sometimes these can be uncomfortable and undesirable to us. We must, however, find healthy ways to deal with our inner child and nurture that part of us, for if we disown that part of ourselves and not deal with it, we will deny a very real and important part of ourselves.

The good news is that the child within us produces many pleasures too, like playfulness and spontaneity. These are positive, desirable traits and help us to genuinely relax and have fun, so it is important to acknowledge all aspects of our inner child.

After all, feeling good about ourselves is a process of becoming more aware of what is going on for us, inside and outside.

Often we keep ourselves from finding out more about who we are and what we feel because it is too painful and we don't want to find out about ourselves for fear that we won't like what we discover. However, we need to search for clarity and respect reality whether pleasant or painful.

One exercise that is great for self-acceptance is very difficult but very powerful in helping us to acknowledge reality and focus on the present:

Stand in front of a mirror naked and look at yourself. Some parts are easier to look at than others for most people so focus on the parts that you feel are pleasant to look at. Focus, take some deep breaths and repeat to yourself five times, "I accept who I am at this moment fully and totally. I see myself now in the present and I do not deny any part of me." Next, move to other parts of your body that are not quite as pleasant to look at and repeat the

50

process. Do this every morning when you awaken. You will be pleasantly surprised that as you do your exercise, you will become more and more aware of yourself in a sincere sense. You will also gain a new respect for reality because this is real and it is what it is. Once you see it as it is, you will experience the importance of the relationship between self-awareness and self-esteem. A mind that honors sight honors itself. Also, if there are things that we wish to change, we have to acknowledge their reality before we can actually do anything about them.

Please understand that self-esteem is not a function of physical attractiveness. The previous exercise is being used to show the link of our willingness to see ourselves as we really are and our ability to change. To accept ourselves is to accept the fact that what we think, feel and do are all expressions of the self at the time they occur. Every moment is new. Every moment provides an opportunity for growth and change.

So, all in all, our goal is to have a strong positive self-concept and to be able to maintain it regardless of approval or disapproval from any other person.

Also, the way we think about our behavior and the standards by which we judge it are very important to our self-esteem.

We are often inclined to condemn ourselves and feel guilty about certain actions, but feeling guilty only lessens our self-esteem.

Sometimes we feel guilt when we violate standards that are not our own but that we took over from other people. Sometimes we feel guilt when we violate our own standards.

Think of an action that you have taken or not taken that badly impacted your self-esteem. Then ask yourself, by whose standards am I judging myself? Are they mine or someone else's? What do I really believe about this issue? If you can carefully examine your feelings with total honesty and in full consciousness see nothing wrong with your behavior, you may find the courage to stop condemning yourself at this point; maybe even gain a new perspective of how you access your behavior.

The bottom line is that a negative feeling about yourself is a self-fulfilling prophecy. It leads to negative behavior. We do not improve by telling ourselves that we are terrible. Our actions are a reflection of who and what we are or think we are so we need to learn an alternative response when we judge that we have behaved poorly. Instead of collapsing into self-damnation, we need to learn to ask, what were the circumstances? Why did my choice or decision seem desirable or necessary in the context? What was I trying to take care of?

Even if the path we choose is mistaken, even if objectively we are engaged in self-destruction, subjectively at some level, we are always trying to take care of ourselves. We need to understand that.

Allowing for the fact that sometimes there are special circumstances requiring special considerations, there are, generally speaking, steps we can take to free ourselves from guilt:

First of all, own the fact that it is we who have taken the particular action. Then, if another person has been harmed by our action, acknowledge to that person the harm we have done and convey our understanding of the consequences of our behavior.

Next, take any and all actions available that might make amends or minimize the harm we have done, such as paying back stolen money, retracting a lie, etc.

Finally, make a firm commitment to behave differently in the future because without a change in behavior, we will continue to create self-distrust.

One of the worst mistakes we can make is to tell ourselves that it is OK to feel guilty. Harshness toward ourselves leaves us inactive and takes away our power. It does not help us, it hurts us. Suffering is stifling and keeps us in a negative place. In order to be truly happy, we need to work toward freeing ourselves from guilt. That takes courage and a desire to live responsibly, honestly and in the here and now. It can be done and it is well worth it.

Always remember that men and women who enjoy high self-esteem live active lives. They take responsibility for their actions and they are involved in problem-solving, not blame. They search for solutions and work toward implementing those solutions.

In summation, self-esteem is a function of being honest with yourself and others, taking responsibility for your actions, acknowledging truth and staying focused in the present.

Self-esteem requires self-acceptance. That means we are true to our feelings and our thoughts. We acknowledge all parts of ourselves, and we don't deny or disown any part. This includes our feelings, emotions, physical characteristics, and actions.

In order to have a healthy self-esteem, we need to make certain that we judge ourselves by our own standards, not the standards of others, no matter how much we love or respect them. We have to develop a self-love that is strong enough to allow us to respect our own standards most.

In matters where we truly feel appropriately guilty, we need to take specific steps to resolve the guilt, rather than suffer passively.

We need to live active lives, not passive ones, taking responsibility for our choices, feelings, and actions. We need to take responsibility for our own existence.

How can we begin to feel better about ourselves? By living in the present, by accepting ourselves and being honest about who we are and where we are in the present. We can also feel better about ourselves if we live responsibly.

What are the rewards? Greater self-trust, and greater self-love, greater joy in our own being, and greater pride in what we have personally achieved.

Also, your positive esteem will show in your face, your mannerisms and your basic way of talking and moving. You will notice yourself being able to speak well of your positive attributes as well as your areas that need nurturing or improvement. You will be a better listener and think about other's opinions and take them into consideration instead of dismissing them right away. You will also be able to acknowledge your own mistakes and work toward correcting them. This will be a reality that you will be able to accept. You will also feel good about who you are because you are not trying to be someone other than yourself or someone that others want you to be.

You will be more open and curious and feel more at ease about trying new things and having new adventures.

You will be quicker to speak up to people and to better defend your positions on things. You will also be more able to understand the need for certain changes in your life and you will have an easier time dealing with the changes.

You will find that you enjoy the humorous aspects of life in yourself and in others. You will be more flexible in responding to challenges, moved by a spirit of adventiveness and even playfulness since you trust your mind and see life in a more realistic and positive manner.

You will still experience times of conflict, crisis, tough decision-making, etc. but you will see yourself as having far more resources to deal with the crisis because of your higher level of self-esteem.

So, all in all, take some time to work on making your esteem even higher than it is at the present and you will experience great and wondrous rewards.

Chapter Four

Self-preparation is the key to a positive, healthy relationship with another.

****

It is a fact that, before you can bring another person into your life, you need to feel good about who you are, your capabilities, strengths and uniqueness.

You are a unique being, the genetic result of your ancestral past. There was only one combination of people over centuries of time who could have led to your existence. Don't you think that makes you special?

What would you like to do to make your life even more special and fulfilling than it is? The choice is yours. Sadly, there are people whose lives consist of nothing but working at unfulfilling jobs by day and watching mindless television by night. When it comes to being effective, they have reached dead ends.

Yet, there are many other people who give meaning to their existence by subjecting themselves to new experiences on all of life's levels. They seek and obtain fulfilling jobs, meaningful relationships, solid education's, stimulating physical activities and rewarding social activities. Their lives are interesting.

What type of person are you and what type of person would you like to be? You can be any type of person you'd like, provided you're willing to do the work that will take you there.

Your education will have a strong impact on what you do. If you don't like the direction in which you are going, you can change it with additional education. People interested in being the best that they can be, realize that education is a life-long process. They realize that knowledge is power and learning is powerful and they pursue as much education as possible, whether through reading, taking courses or talking with interesting, knowledgeable people.

As far as experience is concerned, we grow as a result of education, whether it's obtained in the classroom or through life experiences.

Are you satisfied with the direction in which your life is going? If so, continue on that path and continue to grow. However, if you feel something is missing and you want to improve the quality of your life, the first thing you need to do is think about who you are inside and outside.

Sit down and make a list of all of the qualities that sincerely make up who you are as a person. Think of your physical self, your mental self, your spiritual self and your professional self. As you are making your list, have categories for each of them. Be honest and list who you really are. Use words like, athletic, responsible, open-minded, controlling, procrastinator, etc. Make a partial list and add to it as you think of more characteristics which truly describe you. Do not list the fact that you are a wife, husband, boss, teacher, etc., only words that make up who you are, not certain roles you might play.

Once you have made your lists, look at each category and pick out the characteristics that you feel are positive and healthy. Place a star by those characteristics. Then find the ones that are creating challenges in your life and put a plus sign by them.

Learn to see the challenges as plusses because they will be the catalysts for movement and change. Work on the plusses one at a time in order to make improvements in your life. For instance, if you are a procrastinator, take that plus and learn to turn it into a star. Remember, it takes at least 60 solid days to turn a plus into a star. During those 60 days, you are challenging yourself daily without fail and working on permanent transitions. After 60 days, if you have completed your tasks, you can change your plus to a star, but you must continue to work on it. You will then be ready to move to the next plus and work to make that plus into a star.

Be aware that you might have set-backs. That's normal, natural and all part of winning. The important thing is that you do not allow your setbacks to turn into defeats.

Here are some suggestions to help you as you work to get yourself in top form, physically, emotionally and spiritually:

Exercise Regularly

Many people think exercise benefits only the physical self. While there is no denying that exercise makes us physically fit, it also offers rich benefits for our mental and emotional states.

When we exercise, we strengthen our cardiovascular systems, burn off excess calories and, depending on the activity, we also build muscle. At the same time, the activity stimulates our brains, which secrete endorphins, a natural chemical that can produce a natural high and a feeling of well-being. Believe me, it would take a lot of effort to maintain a mentally or emotionally depressed state after a vigorous exercise session.

Health experts advise that three 20 to 30 minute exercise sessions per week can go a long way toward helping you feel good about yourself. However, keep in mind that this is a minimum. Most of us need to do more.

As for the type of exercise, that's entirely up to you but make sure you include some cardiovascular exercise in your routine, along with some stretching, toning and proper warm up's and cool down's. Also, your form of exercise must be fun if you want to maintain it indefinitely. For example, if you hate to jog, do not take up jogging because you probably will not keep it up for long (unless you learn to like it). There are all kinds of alternative exercises, including swimming, aerobics, biking, dancing or weight-lifting, just to name a few.

If you have not worked out in a while, you might want to start out by walking short distances, then working up to longer distances and eventually to speed walking and a little jogging if you like. I personally enjoy step aerobics and I do two step classes per week and walk on a treadmill once a week. I also do abdominal exercises, stretching and some light free-weight lifting. I have been working out for many years so I can do an hour and a half step class with no problem but I had to work up to that. So will you, if you are a beginner.

You might consider joining a health club or hiring a trainer to get you started. These motivational techniques are great and once you start, you will feel so good, you will make it part of your regular routine. As a matter of fact, if you put off working out, you will feel that you have let yourself down and that will motivate you to begin again.

Stick to a Sensible Diet

It is so difficult to stick to a sensible, healthy diet today. Our lives are so busy and we are running so much that we depend on fast food and restaurant food more than ever. It is normal and natural for us to grab a "quick bite" here and there just to keep us from starving.

Well, obviously, we are going to continue to be busy. We might even get busier so what can we do to create a healthy, sensible diet for ourselves? The answers are not easy and will take a bit of effort on your part but here are a few suggestions:

1. Always start your day with breakfast. Eat before you leave home in the morning or pack it and take it with you. Make breakfast simple, easy and quick. This way, you will be more willing to stick to this regimen.

*Keep healthy breakfast foods on hand such as quick oatmeal which can be mixed with fresh fruit or lite canned fruit, packed in it's own juice.

*Eat fortified cereals with whole wheat or bran with skim milk and fresh fruit.

*Eat whole wheat toast also but make sure your bread package says whole wheat, not just wheat.

*Bake fat-free or low fat muffins from scratch. They are so easy. Just find your favorite recipe and change the ingredients to make them healthy. For instance, instead of butter or margarine, use mashed ripe bananas, fat-free yogurt or applesauce. Also, use egg substitute or egg whites for real eggs. Instead of heavy cream, use evaporated skimmed milk and instead of oil, use half applesauce, half buttermilk or skim milk. Make these muffins on the weekend or during a free evening and freeze half. They are easy to grab in the morning along with a piece of fresh fruit.

2. Pack your own lunch and make it healthy with salads and low-fat sandwiches. Add some fresh fruit and fresh raw veggies with yogurt for dipping.

*If you cannot pack lunch, take time to choose healthy selections from menus. For dessert, have sorbet' or fresh fruit.

*These selections are available at most restaurants and even fast food places are now featuring salad's, fat-free muffins, etc.

*If you must have a burger, choose a small one and instead of putting mayonnaise on it, ask for lettuce, tomatoes and honey mustard sauce. The honey-mustard sauce is lower in fat.

*Skip the fries and have a baked potato with chives instead.

3. For dinner, keep meals simple and as pure as possible. Instead of meals from cartons or cans, make fresh selections as often as possible.

*Have lean cuts of fresh meat, chicken, fish or whatever you desire.

*Add fresh or freshly frozen vegetables and brown rice.

*Boiled, steamed or baked potatoes are a good selection also.

*Eat a variety of different foods but keep meals easy and keep your preparation time short.

*Use left-overs and do quick heat-ups when you can.

(Note: Save special meals which require a lot of preparation time for weekends, holidays and special occasions.)

4. Eat healthy snacks.

*Find fat-free and salt-free foods that are tasty. I really enjoy salt-free baked tortillas. I also enjoy fat-free sorbet' and yogurt bars as well as yogurt, fruit and granola.

*Make your own trail mix from dried fruits and healthy granola. (Note: All granola is not healthy. Read the ingredients and stay away from any palm or palm kernel oils.)

5. Try not to overeat. No matter how good the food is, stop eating when you begin to feel full. There is more on this later in the chapter.

6. Drink six to eight glasses of water each day. If you have trouble reaching your daily quota, here are a few suggestions:

*Go to a Weight Watchers facility and buy their 32 ounce sipping cup. Fill it in the morning and sip all during the day. If you fill this container twice each day and drink all of the water, you will have reached your quota. Of course, you may use any 32 ounce sipping cup. I personally like theirs because it has measurement lines and numbers on it and you can actually see how much you drank.

*Take the 32 ounce cup and put 1/4 cup of fruit juice in the bottom. Fill the rest with water. This gives your water some flavor. Try white grape juice. It is a delicious choice.

*Add some lemon or lime slices.

Whatever it takes to get the water down, do it. It will keep your system cleansed and help to wash out impurities. It will also help your organs function better.

Remember, the food you eat is fuel to keep your body functioning. If you eat sensibly, you will perform more efficiently and feel much better. After all, the human body was built to last approximately 120 years but the reason most of us never get close to living that long is because we do not take proper care of our bodies.

Taking good care of your body through proper diet and exercise will ensure longevity but it will also help you feel good which will allow you to fully enjoy your life.

A physician once told me that the only proven path to longevity was undereating. I thought about this and started to believe it because I know that when I overeat, I feel miserable and my body has to work extra hard to feel good again. I automatically want to lie down and wait for the unpleasant feeling to pass and I always promise never to do it again. Of course I do, but now, I do it less and less and I am very in tune with what I am feeling as I eat because I hate that overstuffed feeling.

When you think of what the doctor told me about undereating, it makes a lot of sense. For example, think of how light you feel when you stop eating before you are full. You have more energy and you function better. This must be the basis of that fact because if you undereat, you have more energy and your body does not have to perform rigorously to help you function again. Also, your body would naturally rid itself of excess fat because you are not adding extra calories and fat which cause weight gain.

This fact is not meant to encourage people to undereat to a point of not eating enough. When I think of undereating, I think of eating until you are satisfied and not full. That means eating a sensible amount of food to provide the nutrition you need and stopping before you feel uncomfortable or full. Try it at your next meal, no matter how good the food is. Stop before you are uncomfortably full and notice the difference.

In summation, in order to look and feel our best, we need to load up on fruits, vegetables, fiber, fish, low-fat dairy products and lots of water. We need to stay in tune with our bodies as we are eating and try not to overeat. If we do this, we will be providing our bodies with the fuel they need to function properly for longer periods of time.

Keep your Stress Level in Tact

Stress can certainly be the root of many of our health problems, but in recent years it has been blamed for diseases like cancer and hypertension and considered one of the causes of drug and alcohol abuse.

Stress is also a natural response to external demands. Normal stress is what keeps life exciting and challenging. Studies have shown that normal stress levels can stimulate the immune system instead of suppressing it.

Stress can be a positive factor, giving us the edge we need to perform at our peak. Examples of positive stress might include the challenge of a new job, beginning college, getting married, or performing on stage for the first time.

The difference between positive and negative stress has a great deal to do with our own perceptions of it. What one person sees as an exciting challenge might be seen by someone else as a burden or a threat.

Some personality types are more likely to become stressed than others. People who are negative, pessimistic and judgmental are more likely to suffer the adverse effects of stress. Those who are able to take a more positive approach to life's events are less susceptible to the harmful effects of stress.

How affected are you by everyday stress?

*Are you always in a hurry?

*Do you often lose your temper?

*Do you feel guilty when you are not doing something?

*Do you have trouble sleeping?

*Do you like to be in control of things?

*Are you usually the one who does the job best?

If you answered yes to many of these questions, you probably experience stress on a regular basis. If this is true, you need to find healthy ways to eliminate some of this before it begins to take a toll on your mental health.

Each of us perceives the world in our own way. Some people are able to go through life without letting much of anything bother them. They are able to shrug off daily annoyances and let them go. Others are frequently upset and have a tendency to critically evaluate their own performance and the performances of those around them. Most people fall somewhere in the middle, but we all have something that "drives us crazy."

One of the most common reactions to stressful situations is a change in breathing pattern. You may have found yourself holding your breath or breathing very shallow when you are in a stressful situation. This type of breathing affects you both mentally and physically. The breath not only brings oxygen into the system, carrying vital energy to every cell in the body, it also carries waste products like carbon dioxide out of the system.

Shallow breathing, then, not only reduces the amount of oxygen to vital organs like the brain, but it allows toxins and waste to remain in the bloodstream.

In a stressful situation, remembering to breathe properly can have a significant effect on the whole body. By filling the lungs and breathing calmly for a few minutes, more oxygen gets to the brain and muscles, more toxins are eliminated from your system, and tense muscles begin to relax. The heart responds by beating in rhythm with your slow and steady breathing. A calmer heart will make you mentally calmer and better able to deal with whatever crisis is at hand.

The next time you find yourself in a stressful situation, focus on your breathing. Are you holding your breath or taking short, shallow breaths? Consciously begin to take deeper, slower breaths. Over the next several days, become aware of how you breathe in different situations. How are you breathing right now?

Here is an exercise that will increase oxygen flow and relax the body. It is an excellent technique to use when you are feeling upset or having difficulty centering yourself.

Sitting comfortably, breathe through your nose counting slowly up to six. Exhale through the nose, counting slowly to twelve. Let the air fill your lungs as you inhale and exhale as gently as possible. Don't force the air. Do this for one minute.

Become aware of how you feel. Are you calmer? More relaxed? Does your body feel more loose? If so, you can use this exercise when you need to relax, especially in moments of high-level stress. Taking deep, slow, even breaths can re-energize and relax you and have an overall positive effect on your emotional as well as your physical state.

Laughter also helps us take deeper breaths. A good, deep, solid laugh that brings you to tears can do wonders for muscle tension too. It massages deep muscles that may never be reached otherwise and it improves circulation around vital organs. Laughter increases breathing and oxygen exchange and it may stimulate the body to produce endorphins, the body's natural pain killers.

Research has also shown that facial muscles can affect the emotions, so that just by smiling, you can improve your outlook and lift your spirits. Smiling is a great way to release tension and you may want to try it when you're in the middle of a tense situation, a situation where smiling is the last thing you would naturally do. Even just imagining yourself smiling can help.

Just by laughing or smiling, our perceptions can automatically change, making it much easier to deal with stressful situations. Try it for yourself right now:

Sitting quietly, think of something very pleasant. It could be anything from a warm, sunny beach to a romantic evening out with someone special. Allow yourself to feel this. Put yourself there and feel yourself begin to smile. Try to concentrate and focus on the feeling and where it is coming from. Allow this feeling to course through your entire body. Stay with this awareness for several minutes. It is guaranteed to relax you and take you to a new level.

These are the kinds of things we can do for ourselves to get through stressful times. They are not long term solutions but they certainly can help. Being the mature adults that we are, we know we cannot solve all of our problems through laughter and deep breathing. They simply can eliminate the distress that prevents us from being our best, which is exactly what we need to be when overcoming the obstacles that life all too often presents.

All in all, you need to be the best that you can be at this time and you need to continue to work on the many aspects of yourself which are truly you.

When you are feeling good and positive about yourself and your energy level is in a good place, you are then ready to seek relationships with others and, hopefully the ultimate relationship with another person.

However, you must always remember that the first and most important relationship is with yourself and you will always need to strive toward being true to yourself.

The next chapter will help you in your search to find a good partner, whether you seek love, marriage, friendship, companionship, some of the above, or all of the above.

Chapter Five

Now that I'm ready, where do I find quality people to go out with?

****

Once you begin to feel confident and ready to meet individuals, please understand that this is a process that takes time, patience and studying on your part. Your intuition has to be keen and you really need to listen to what you are feeling inside at all times. It takes a serious commitment and can be very time consuming.

I had been working with Sheila for quite a few weeks because she had suffered a loss through a relationship she had with a commitmentphobe. She was devastated when he finally left her and she came to me for counseling. Commitmentphobia is a difficult thing to deal with and we will discuss it later in the book.

We will also talk about how to recognize a commitmentphobe.

Anyway, Sheila had worked through the grieving process and was finally ready to meet new people.

I let her know, first of all, that meeting new people was a process and that it could be as demanding as a part-time job. I also let her know that all of her work could pay off so well that she would easily forget all of the work she had put into it. I told her that it was all in the way she looked at it. If she saw it as a grueling task, she would burn out quickly and possibly even give up, but, if she looked at it as fun and properly paced herself, she would enjoy every step.

If you are a person who is fresh out of a relationship, please do not undertake this project. You are not ready. Go back and read Chapter IV. Work on yourself and prepare yourself for a good relationship. Do good things for yourself. Allow yourself to experience the grieving process. Sometimes, this is not pleasant but it is a great time to do many good things for yourself, your family and friends and all of the people who give you unconditional love. Trust me. You will need them during this period.

Most people need weeks to get through the grieving process. Others need months, but if this process takes too long, the person should seek help because they can slip into depression and end up with other problems as a result of what they have gone through. Many times, it depends on how long the actual relationship lasted and how intense and involved the relationship was.

For Sheila, she was only in the relationship for three months, but she had incorporated much of her life with his and they were discussing marriage and had begun doing things with each other's children. She was so crushed and hurt that, even though the relationship was short-lived, it took her quite a few months to work through it.

When I speak of the grieving process, I am speaking of the same process we use when we have experienced a loss through death. When we end a love relationship, it is like a death because we experience the loss and our lives change just as if a loved one had died. That's why it is extremely important to allow yourself to go through and experience the grieving process.

The grieving process consists of stages you must go through when a relationship ends. The stages are as follows:

1. Shock   2. Denial   3. Anger   4. Depression
5. Understanding   6. Acceptance

Each of these stages requires time. Some people say that the only thing they felt when their relationship was over was relief. I take them back to when they were in the relationship and help them understand that their grieving had taken place while they were actually in the relationship. Consequently, when the relationship ended, they felt relieved and were ready to go on with their lives.

It is important that people are able to identify what is going on because some people will stay in the denial stage and think they are fine and ready for a new relationship when really they are not. They want to deaden the pain but this is not good because it will cause problems in the new relationship.

When my friends and I are gathering clothes to contribute to the battered women's shelter, I always say to the ones who hesitate to give up some of their old pieces; "Clean out the old stuff so you can make room for some great new stuff." This is true in relationships. If we don't relax and take time to clean up the old wounds, we will take all of that negative baggage into the next relationship and, even though some of those relationships work out, it makes the journey much harder. So, take the time to grieve before you get back out there.

I currently own and operate a company called Matters of the Heart, Inc. and we do several things. We offer seminars to help people who have been out of the dating game for a while. We show them how and where to meet new people. We also offer introduction services where we put people together through match-making and we write personal ads for individuals. We do pre-marital seminars, esteem building seminars and various types of support groups. Overall, we do all types of relationship consulting, so our main focus is helping people obtain and maintain healthy, mature relationships.

Here are some of the things we use in our seminars for people who are trying to meet others, in order to form new relationships. We tell them that "once you are ready to venture out, you need to do several things:"

*Contact all of your friends, relatives, co-workers and close neighbors. Let them know that you are looking for quality individuals to date. Be specific and let them know what type of person you are looking for. This works for a lot of people and can get you some great dates.

*When you're out running errands, always look your best because, when you look your best, you feel most confident and you will be more open to saying hi to people you are attracted to, maybe even starting conversation's. Remember, many people meet in grocery stores, drug stores, post office lines and other non-traditional places. All you need is a smile, an open mind and the nerve to say hello and, as hard as this may seem to be, you will feel much more confident if you look your best.

TIP: Some great places to meet ladies are lingerie shops, women's stores, women's departments at large department stores, craft stores, aerobics classes, book stores, etc.

Some great places to meet men are: hardware stores, car dealerships, auto shows, boat shows, men's clothing stores, sports events, computer classes, computer stores, etc.

Be aware, however, that the above mentioned places are not exclusively male or female oriented. Lots of women attend sporting events and lots of men take aerobics classes. These are just basic leads.

Be creative. Come up with your own personal lists and get out there and meet people.

*Spend some time in restaurants, restaurant lounges and coffee shops. Single people are always there, especially coffee shops. If you are hesitant to do this alone, take a book, newspaper or something interesting to read.

If you spot a potential prospect, watch that person and when you catch their eye, smile and continue to read, then, make eye contact again and smile again. After a while, motion for them to join you, or motion to them asking if you can join them. If they are reading something, you can always strike up a conversation about what they are reading.

*Place a personal ad. Many people frown on personal ads. They say that a person has to be "desperate" to place or answer a personal ad. This could be true. People could very well be desperately seeking a companion, but is this a bad thing? I don't think so. This is not bad or negative and it could turn into something very positive including a very fulfilling relationship, even marriage. It's all right to make a move because you desperately want a companion. It's not all right, however, if you don't go through the proper screening process. That's the mistake a lot of people make and the consequences end up creating despair, confusion and negative feelings about the entire process.

Remember, feeling desperate is not bad, because it can jump-start you into necessary action to reach positive results. However, desperate behavior, such as answering a personal ad and going to a strangers house, etc. is not good and can lead to destruction and despair.

During one of my seminars on ways to meet single individuals, I met a beautiful woman named Gwen. She was divorced for the second time and quite discouraged about how to meet people. She was an entrepreneur and worked alone so she did not meet new people very often at her place of business. To add to this, she worked six days a week until late at night so she did not have time to go out to meet people. When she came to me and told me her story, I took out my appointment book and set up a coaching session with her.

When she came in, we talked for a while and once I learned more about her situation, I totally understood how she felt. I realized that the best way for her to meet people would be to place a personal ad.

When I suggested this to her, she said, "My God, what will my children think? What will my friends think? Won't they think I am crazy and desperate?"

I explained to her that many people do not understand the process very well and they might think negative thoughts so I suggested that she try the process first, get her feet wet, then let her family and friends know later. She agreed.

She contracted the company to write her personal ad and she ran it three times in a local newspaper. She did not get a lot of responses because her ad was specific and she asked for exactly what she wanted. She followed the guidelines which she had learned in the seminar and went out with four men before she met Jim. I am happy to report that after dating for almost a year, the two of them are engaged to be married.

Let me tell you how you can make the experience of placing a personal ad a positive experience:

+Write an honest personal ad. Represent yourself well. If you are tall, say that. If you have red hair, say that. If you are a single Mom or Dad, say that. If you want a long-term relationship, say that. If you want someone to golf with, say that. Learn to be specific and ask for exactly what you want and/or do not want. If you want a non-smoker, say that, etc.

You must understand, however, that the more specific you are, the less answers you will receive. This is good, not bad because you know who you are and the kind of person you are looking for. If you want more responses however, be less specific. It's up to you.

Also, you can run your ad in different ways. Maybe, run one ad worded a special way, then run another ad the next month worded another way. Most newspapers will allow you to place an ad free, so place it over and over and do not stick to one paper. Research, find newspapers in and around your area offering this service and take advantage of it.

+Set a realistic goal, stick to it and when you feel tired or burned out, take a break, try something different, then go back and try again. Trust me, you will know when you are ready to take a break.

+Once you decide to start calling your prospects back, call your local phone company and get a block put on the phone so that people with caller I.D. will not have your last name and/or telephone number. It's important for you to remain anonymous until or unless you feel O.K. giving more information. This gives you power and control over the situation and you can make the decisions that feel good to you. If you cannot place a block on your phone, go to your local Kinko's,

Copy Max or other comfortable public place where they have courtesy phones. You can make your calls there as long as you keep them short. You can continue to do this until you feel comfortable enough to give out your number. Of course, pay phones in malls and parking lots are good also.

+In order to screen the person, ask questions, then check them out. For instance, ask where a person works, call up and verify. Ask for an address or street name. Drive by to see if the neighborhood looks safe. Ask a person whether or not he or she is divorced and has any children. If you do not feel confident with the answers you are given, remember, marriage, divorce and child birth records are public information. However, I would not advise you to look through a persons records unless you discuss it with the person and they have no objections. If you feel you have to get information without letting the person know, there is something wrong and you need to think about whether or not you want to continue this quest.

+Trust your gut feelings. If something feels weird or wrong over the phone or even in person, do not continue this quest. Go on to the next person.

+Once you have spoken with a person on the phone several times and you are feeling extremely comfortable, take it to the next step. Arrange a meeting at a public place, well lit and with lots of people around. Plan to meet for an hour and if things do not go well, you can make your exit quickly.

+Never leave with the person. Always say your good-byes, excuse yourself, go to the restroom, then after you come out, go and have another cup of coffee to make sure the person is gone. For extra safety, go to a place where you can valet park. Make sure your date is held during the day when there is plenty of light and make sure no one is following you when you leave the place where you have met the person.

+You may choose to have someone drop you off and pick you up. It's safe and make's for great conversation on the way home. You might also have a friend drive you there and wait on the other side of the room, then take you home after the date.

+When you meet the person, always have an identifying object. At Matters of the Heart, we like to use the color red. For instance, if you are meeting someone for the first time, tell them you will have something red in your hand. They are to do the same. This is a great conversation starter. You can tell the story of what you are holding, where it came from, etc.

+Continue to meet the person in public places for a while. Be patient and take it slow. Get to know the person and enjoy your times together. This is safe and lots of fun.

Let me emphasize that I am not trying to scare people and make them fearful of these processes, however, I feel that the reason there is such a stigma attached to non-traditional ways of meeting people is the issue of safety.

Very often, when you decide to meet someone in a non-traditional way, some people will say, "Be careful. You don't know that person. What if he's and ax murderer, or what if she is a dangerous person?" People are fearful and sometimes that's good because it keeps them safe and keeps them from doing foolish things, but often it keeps them from doing anything at all and that's not good if they want to meet others. That's why, in our seminars and in this book, I am letting people know what they need to know to be safe, but also, to use this information and go out and take some "safe risks." The only guarantee is that if you don't try something, you won't gain anything.

*Use introduction services. There are so many out there now and they each have different formats. If you prefer to look through pictures and biographies, there are service's set up this way. There are also services that do all the work for you. You just tell them what you want and they will send profiles to you monthly.

Tip: Visit these places, meet with a representative or have a thorough phone conversation with someone and get all of your questions answered. Figure out what type of service you want. Do you want to do all the work by looking through biographies and pictures or do you want to fill out a one-time survey and questionnaire and trust them to do the matching for you? It's all personal preference. How much money do you have or are you willing to spend on a service? Remember, when you are trying to meet new people, you need to do a variety of things, so make sure you find a service that does not cost a fortune so that you can do other things also.

Call your Better Business Bureau, ask around town and find the best service at a price that is comfortable for you.

*Join clubs and organizations. For instance, if you like to ski or want to learn to ski, join a club. If you like playing tennis, join a tennis club or health club that has tennis facilities. There are several singles groups you can join, including church groups.

*Take a dance class. It can be anything from ballroom dancing to line dancing.

*Surf the Net. Many people are finding love and meeting new friends through their personal computer. Explore this possibility. It can be a lot of fun.

There are other ways to meet people, but these are some great ways to get you started.

Just remember, have fun and take a break when you start to burn out. Get back in the game when you feel ready.

Who knows, you could develop some great friendships, have tons of fun or even find your partner for life.

Chapter Six

The Dating Game

****

Many people approach dating cautiously. There are so many stories about dates from hell, many people just say, what's the use?

I've even heard people say things like, "I would love to find a great partner and get married, I just don't want to have to go out on dates."

I've also heard people tell jokes about dating. One man said, "The only reason I married her is so I wouldn't have to go out on those damn dates anymore." Well, as the crowd roared with laughter, it was obvious that his wife was not amused. She just went along with it as part of a joke. Hopefully, they communicated about her discomfort when they got home later, or even on the way home.

I can remember when I was in high school. Dating was so much fun and so appealing. We all looked forward to our weekend dates and we had so much fun.

When a special person asked us out, we were thrilled and could not wait to share the news and figure out what to wear. We called our best buddies the second the date was over.

Times have changed, but not for everyone. I still have girlfriends who call me after their dates and we still have fun getting prepared for these dates.

I feel that a big part of the solution to this difficulty comes from changing the way we talk and think about it. If you view dating as the process of courtship, as a way for two people to get to know each other in order to build trust, respect, and love, then courtship can indeed be a great experience. It can lead to commitment and can be a process that is just plain fun.

It's clear that you will not find everyone you date attractive or a potential partner. But it's also clear that many people make judgments too hastily. They look for instant proof that someone they've just met or are seeing for the first time is "the one." Some ladies have even told me that they put their first name with the guy's last name after the first date to see how it sounds. This is fine as long as you know that relationships take time to build and grow.

When you meet someone that you are attracted to, you feel great and you feel like it is "magic." That's great as long as you understand that you still need to spend time getting to know the man or woman. This does not mean the "magic" will vanish. It just increases the chance that the man or woman you fall in love with will be Mr. or Ms. Right, not Mr. or Ms. Right Now. That will make the magic even more wonderful and the love between you even greater.

You will also need to take some time to develop a "must have" list. This is a list of all of the things you feel you must have in a relationship. When you make your "must have" list, it should include qualities like:

*spends time with and enjoys my children,

*does not abuse alcohol or drugs,

*is considerate of other's feelings

*is marriage-minded

*is supportive of my choices, both personal and professional.

These are qualities to place on that list, not things such as:

*has to be 6 feet tall

*has to have long blonde hair

These physical characteristics, while great if you like these, will not create a long lasting relationship, only limit your choices.

Ask questions and find out things about the person, things that are important. Use your own set of screening devices to discover whether the person is a potential partner for you or not. Do not be afraid to ask questions about anything you want to know.

When you meet a person, ask that person questions about himself or herself, their friends, family, goals, dreams, etc. In other words, allow the person to talk freely about himself or herself. Be a good listener and learn about this person, but do not listen in a judgmental way. If you hear something that does not feel right to you, question the person about it, if you feel comfortable doing that. Don't let something that bothers you keep you from experiencing that person further. Take note and research it a little further.

98

Let me give you an example. Michael is a great friend of mine. We have known each other for many years and see each other quite often. When he met Barbara, his new wife, he did not want to go out with her after the first date because she told him that she had an 11 year old daughter that she wanted to eventually re-gain custody of. You see, she had consented to allow her ex-husband to raise the child but now that she had gotten her affairs in order, she wanted her daughter back. She explained to Michael that this was one of the things that pained her more than anything, to have to be separated from her daughter.

When Michael came home from the date, he spoke of how good he felt with Barbara. He said that he liked her so much that he could not see her again because she wanted to raise her daughter. You see, Michael had a daughter himself that he had just sent off to college and he was ready to start a new, childless life with a potential partner.

I suggested to Michael that he just go out and enjoy Barbara's company and that he should talk to her about his feelings. Well, he decided to discuss this on the next date, just casually. He explained the joys and pains he had experienced raising his daughter alone for the past seven years and that he did not plan to have other kids or live with kids again. He said that he was at the point in his life where he only wanted to be responsible for himself.

Barbara was quiet about this but always remembered it. Well, seven months later when Michael proposed, he asked Barbara if she would consider going to pre-marital counseling to work through the situation concerning her daughter. She consented and they were able to work through the situation so that it was comfortable for both of them.

Today, Barbara's daughter lives with the two of them three days each week and she lives with her father the rest of the time. They are all quite happy with this arrangement.

The point I am making is clear. Don't dismiss a potential partner because she is 10 pounds over her ideal weight or he is not a bank president. There are a lot of good men and women out there to go around, but there are not enough perfect figured women to go around, just as there are not enough professional athletes and male bank president's to go around. All in all, give people a chance and make your must-have list realistic and workable for you.

My friend Michael's must-have list clearly stated that: she must be childless or have grown children, but he consented to date Barbara and they are currently living happily ever after.

Beware of the commitmentphobe. This is a person who has an exaggerated fear of commitment. I'm sure many of you have been involved with this type of individual at least once in your life.

The commitmentphobe might be the man who doesn't call after a wonderful first date, or the woman who is totally interested in you and leaves after the first night of sex. It may be the boyfriend or girlfriend who finds a way to ruin the relationship just as it heads for marriage, or it may be the woman or man who waits until after marriage to ignore your emotional needs. He or she might become unfaithful or emotionally abusive. When this happens, chances are you are dealing with a person who absolutely has a problem with commitment. To that person, being committed to you or anyone else scares them to death

101

and they eventually leave. You don't understand it. You don't see yourself as threatening. As a matter of fact, you may not even have wanted that much from this particular person. Well, guess what, they probably don't understand their reactions any better than you do. All they know is that the relationship is "too close for comfort." Something about it and something about you makes them anxious.

If the fear is strong enough, the commitmentphobe will ultimately sabotage, destroy or run away from anyone who represents "happily ever after." In other words, if their fear is too great, the commitmentphobe will not be able to love, no matter how much he or she wants to.

But that's not how it seems in the beginning. In the beginning of the relationship, each time you look at this person, you see someone who needs and wants love. They display their vulnerabilities and let down their guard so easily. They show their sensitive side right away and make you feel that it is "safe" to become close to them.

But, guess what? As soon as you allow yourself to become close and as soon as you are willing to give love a chance and move the relationship forward, something changes. Suddenly the person begins running away, either figuratively, by withdrawing, or literally, by disappearing and never calling again. Either way, you are left with disappointed dreams and destroyed self-esteem. What happened, what went wrong, and why is this scenario so familiar to so many people?

One beautiful Sunday morning in May, Karen was sitting in church enjoying a wonderful sermon. She was especially happy this Sunday because she and her boyfriend had decided to get married and she was there to ask the minister if he would perform the ceremony. After church, she asked the minister and he said yes, congratulated her and proceeded to give her a tour of possible reception facilities.

She was about to make her exit when a very handsome young man approached her. He extended his hand and introduced himself. He said, "Hello, my name is David Wilson and I overheard you say you were getting married. Congratulations! He's a very lucky man. I also heard that you were looking to do some volunteer work and I do a lot of charity work in the area. If you ever want to volunteer, please call me." He gave Karen his card and she walked away very impressed.

When Karen got home from church that day, she couldn't help but think of the young man who had approached her, mainly because she was having some difficulties with her boyfriend Marlon. You see, he had not officially proposed and she did not have a ring, though they had mutually agreed on a date for the ceremony. Also, he was not spending much time with her lately and she was feeling a bit uneasy.

Anyway, she did call David because she wanted to volunteer to do some work and get her mind off of her troubles. He was delighted to hear from her and asked her to accompany him to a big affair that was being held that same weekend. Karen was flattered but knew that she should not attend because of her relationship but when she asked Marlon about his weekend plans, he told her that he was going away. This did not feel right to Karen, so she called David back and he convinced her to accompany him as a friend. She went, had a great time and was totally captivated by David's charm. She began to see him because Marlon was spending less and less time with her. She ended up canceling the wedding and breaking up with Marlon.

This seemed to be exactly what David wanted and things seemed to be going well. David introduced her to all of his family, including his parents, brothers, sisters and his children. He took her to many grand functions and he told her that he wanted to marry her the following year. They had even looked at wedding rings.

Then, all of a sudden, David stopped calling her every day. He went out of town a couple of times and she could not get in touch with him. She would leave messages for him but he would not return her calls and when she would finally talk with him, he would apologize and say that he was going through some family problems and they were too personal to explain.

Well, needless to say, Karen was devastated and she knew the relationship was over so when she demanded that he come over to tell her, she had gone through several of the stages of grief already. When he finally admitted that it was over, he had a really hard time telling her. He had avoided it but Karen eventually forced him to say it.

When she came to me and told me the story, I explained to her that she, unfortunately, had gotten involved with a commitmentphobe. I told her to buy the book, <u>Men Who Can't Love</u> by Steven Carter and Julia Sokol. This is a wonderful guide to learn how to recognize a commitmentphobe.

Because commitmentphobic people are not easy to spot, I suggest that you take your time with the people you meet. Sometimes these types of people can seem so sincere but when you get too close, they will pull away and totally break your heart.

Karen learned her lesson and it took her several months to get over this heartache and heartbreak, even though the relationship with David was only a total of four months.

I am happy to report, however, that she and Marlon became friends again, went into couples counseling with his minister and were married a year later. The last I heard, they were planning to start a family. So, you see, this story ended happily but not without a lot of heartache.

The best advise I, or anyone else can give you is, take your time. Enjoy getting to know a person

106

before you make a physical, mental and/or sexual commitment.

Dating and learning about a person can be so much fun. Do fun, exciting things together. If you feel comfortable, share the dating expenses so that you can do a lot of great things because the more time you spend together doing things, the better you get to know the person.

It is nice to go to fine restaurants, plays and travel to great places, but remember, having quiet dinners at home, watching movies at home or simple walks in the park are important times also. Experience the person in all types of settings in order to get to know the person better.

Once you have spent a sufficient amount of time with a person, (we suggest at least four seasons), you will be better prepared for marriage.

Chapter Seven

Committing to the relationship that feels right

****

Once you have found a person and you want to make a commitment, spend some time getting to know that person. Be prepared to experience the joys and challenges of relationships and understand that problem-free relationships do not exist. All relationships have problems and concerns. You will experience these. They are healthy and prepare you for a life with the person you have chosen.

When you decide to be with someone, put into effect what we call the "two month rule". In other words, take the first two months to see how things feel. Use these months to get to know each other's likes, dislikes, preferences, etc. Spend quality time with the person. This way you can see whether or not the person fits comfortably into your life. However, I must warn you, if you have doubts and questions and have learned things about the person that feel uncomfortable, discuss these issues. If you cannot come to an agreement, do not continue, especially if passion and physical attraction are the only things holding the two of you together.

Evaluate the situation objectively. Talk it over with friends, maybe even a professional and make a decision because if it feels wrong in this short time, it is best to cut your losses and get out now.

You will still need to go through the grieving process, however, the good news is that the grieving period will be shorter and you will be able to work through the stages a little faster. You can then start anew, armed with fresh knowledge about yourself and what you truly want and need in a relationship.

This is very important because if you are looking for a positive, healthy relationship, you do not need to tie yourself down to a person for more than two months if you know the relationship is not healthy and positive for you. Also, if you feel in this amount of time that the relationship has no place to go, move on.

Many people do not move ahead because they feel that they might not find another person or that they will be lonely. Believe me, there are many men and women out here looking for love just as you are and being lonely or alone for a while is a small price to pay for finding the person who is just right for you.

Once you are sure about the person you are with and the two of you decide to work toward marriage, there are some very important issues and subjects you need to discuss and be clear about.

These subjects' are; children, money and sex, because these are probably the top three issues that couples have disputes about.

For instance, if you already have children, do not assume that you know the role your partner will play. Discuss this. Find out what is comfortable for your partner. If you are not comfortable with his or her feelings, discuss this and work on a solution that is comfortable for the two of you. This can be done.

Also, if you want to have children, discuss this and answer the following questions:

110

1. Where will we live once the children begin to come?
2. How many children will we have?
3. Are we each physically able to have children?
4. When will we have them?
5. How will we raise them? (values, education, etc.)
6. How will we discipline them?

This can be a delightful conversation and should lead to some great clarity. If you reach some uncomfortable places while having this conversation, work on these until you both feel better.

Take some time to discuss money. This is a crucial one. Find out how you will pay the bills, who's responsible for what and what's comfortable for each of you. Find out how each person sees money. Are you a saver? Is she more of a person who lives from check to check and spends all of her money? Do you like to invest your money? Does he prefer to put it under the mattress? Who makes more money and who will take on which responsibilities? Will you have a joint account, separate accounts and what money goes into what account and what are these accounts for?

Please do not have "secret" accounts or little "stashes" on the side that your partner does not know about. This is important because, first of all, if you feel you need to have a secret account or stash, this says that you do not trust your partner and if he or she finds out, it will cause some issues of trust to come forth which will have more severe consequences.

Also, psychologically, if you are stashing money away "just in case things don't go well", you are making a statement to yourself that you actually do not believe in the relationship with all your heart and you have doubts. This can eventually become a self-fulfilling prophecy because if you think you might have problems down the road, guess what? You will. You must put yourself in the relationship wholeheartedly and without doubt or you are doomed to failure.

Trust me, I know why we do these things. We have all been bruised and battered, literally and figuratively in relationships and we just want to feel that we are protecting ourselves. While this is a normal reaction, I encourage you to start out fresh

and clean and with no secrets. Then, if you see problems down the road where you need to plan an exit, you might want to make other plans. However, give it 100% and it will totally change your outlook. Give it your all, because here is a powerful equation:
Two people giving 100% = Success.

What about sex? We all remember how it was when we first met each other, how we had visions of swinging from chandeliers and when we got together, all we could think of was getting dinner or the movie over with so that we could go someplace and make passionate love.

Well, as relationships grow and responsibilities come into the equation, things change. We can still have many passionate moments, just maybe not quite as often as in the beginning. Anyway, be clear about your expectations and desires.

I am not suggesting that you sit down and write out a plan of how often you will have sex and which positions and sex toys you will use on which night. I am simply saying, discuss what is important to the two of you concerning sex. Discuss frequency, style, various turn on's and fantasies. Also, decide how you will deal with sexual conflict, should it occur.

Continue to use spontaneity in the sexual part of your relationship and work to keep passion alive.

The ground of a strong and lasting commitment is the passionate connection between two people whose beings say yes to each other. When two people connect being to being, they experience something deep in their soul that goes beyond mere romance or desire. Something powerful and real inside them starts waking up and coming alive in each other's presence.

The deeper a soul-connection goes, however, the more it brings our real selves to the surface. So before two people can feel confident about making a commitment to each other, they need to find out whether they can handle this challenge.

The quality of an honest, loving connection brings out the best and the worst in us. Along with our openheartedness, all our fears, insecurities, and resistance's to intimacy start to emerge. We may find ourselves becoming more emotional, jealous, or unreasonable than we had ever thought possible. We may even seriously doubt whether we have what it takes to make a go of a relationship at all. Real intimacy, in short, brings up our unfinished business and all the rough spots in ourselves and in our partner that still need to be polished, refined, and further developed.

So, although many couples marry purely out of delight in each other, it is necessary for two people to go through a certain amount of disappointment and hard times before making that final leap. That's why we suggest at least four seasons. This gives the couple time to get to know a lot about each other and experience many sides of the other person. You definitely will not and cannot experience all sides of a person in four seasons but it is a good start.

The experiences a couple has during this time provides a way of testing the relationship. Questions should be asked, such as:

*Can the couple handle the disappointment of realizing that they can never meet all of each other's needs?

*Does their relationship depend on a limited set of roles, or can they make room for all their different sides?

*Can they include not just their sweetness and love, but also the thunderstorms that arise between them?

The main question facing a couple when they come up against their rough edges is, can they work with whatever arises between them, no matter how demanding it may be, and include that as part of their path together? If they cannot do this, they may never be fully present in the relationship, and therefore, never fully committed. After all, facing whatever arises and meeting it with attention and concern is necessary, in order to find a way to move through it.

All too often we imagine that we must bend ourselves out of shape to fit into a relationship. For instance, we might think, "Now that I am married, I shouldn't feel any longing for independence, for being alone, or for other deep, intimate friendships." Yet, no matter how committed we are to a relationship, we will continue to feel desires to be alone and attractions to other people. If we try to eliminate such feelings, they will only haunt us, making us regard the relationship as confining, or they may suddenly erupt and come out in inappropriate ways.

We have to continue to be true to our own feelings and our true selves, as we are now and as we change.

Once you have committed to marriage and have begun to blend your lives together, don't forget to keep passion and romance in your life.

Here are only a few suggestions:

1. Continue to have candlelight dinners on occasion. Have stimulating conversation and don't worry about cleaning up the dishes. Enjoy the conversation, even after the meal. Then, retire to the den, curl up together and watch a movie. After the movie, go to bed together and curl up in each others arms to sleep. You will feel very connected, whether this leads to sex or not. The sex, while important, is not the main focus. The intimacy is.

2. Send your partner on a romantic, adventurous treasure hunt. Call your partner and ask if they will stop by a specific florist to pick up some flowers on the way home. Tell them that you have already ordered the flowers. All they have to do is pick them up.

When they get there, have a note waiting for them that says, now, go to the wine shop. I have a nice Merlot waiting there for you. Please pick it up. When he or she gets there, have another note waiting that says, please stop by the Chinese restaurant. Dinner is waiting there for you. Pick it up and bring it to me. Once they get to the restaurant, have a sealed letter for them. In this envelope will be a hotel key and the note will say: Now, bring all these goodies and join me at the Marriot across the street. I'm in room 234.

Seal it in a special way. If you are a woman, use red lipstick and seal it with a kiss. If you are a man, seal it with your favorite cologne that drives her wild when you wear it.

When he or she arrives, greet your mate at the door dressed very seductively and with a sexy smile. Your partner will do the rest.

Of course you will have to pre-plan all of this and it has to be very organized so have fun planning it and watch fireworks explode at the finale.

3. Buy fresh rose petals and when your mate arrives home, have the petals begin at the door and lead up to the bedroom where you are, looking sexy and smelling great. Have rose petals on the freshly made bed and have an ice bucket with champagne. Also have seductive finger foods, such as strawberries and cream, kiwi, finger sandwiches, etc. Let your mate know that the two of you are celebrating the arrival of a King/Queen. Explain to your partner that he or she truly is King or Queen and you just wanted to take a moment to celebrate. Spend the rest of the night convincing your partner that he or she truly is a King or Queen.

4. Give your partner a set of *Love Coupons*. These can be bought through our mail order service at Matters of the Heart or you can make your own. You would give your partner the coupons and let him or her know that they are redeemable at any time. Here is an example of what a coupon might say:

*This coupon entitles you to one hundred of the most sensual kisses you ever experienced from the top of your handsome or beautiful head to the bottom of your precious toes.

Another coupon might be a little racy and say:

*This coupon entitles you to a wildly passionate evening filled with erotic, intense animal-like sex.

5. Take a long Sunday drive. Try to drive along the water, if you live near water. Stop at a great little seafood restaurant and have wine and seductive seafood. Feed each other. Take your time, at least two hours, then drive a little farther and check into al little hotel by the water. Don't worry that you do not have a toothbrush. That's part of the seduction.

6. Make a lunch date with your partner. Meet him or her at a quiet, intimate restaurant where you can look into each others eyes, hold hands and romance each other for a little while. It will truly make the rest of your day exciting and make coming home that night very worthwhile.

7. Call each other during the day just to say, "I love you" or "I miss you". Discuss plans of getting together later and what you would like to do.

8. Write love notes and put them in places where they are sure to be discovered at unexpected times. Some good places are:
    *On a pillow
    *Under the sun visor in the car
    *In the shower
    *In a coat pocket
    *In a purse or briefcase

These make great surprises and are sure to make your partner smile.

9. Stop at a fancy chocolate shop like Godiva or Malley's and pick up a few truffles or other sweet goodies for your mate. The store personnel will wrap the candies in beautiful paper. This is certain to make your partner feel special.

10. Send flowers to your mate's office, place of business, hotel, meeting place, or wherever he or she

might be during the day when there are people. It is always nice to receive flowers when others get to see them also. It makes a person feel very special when others see that someone cares about them.

Make up your own romantic lists. Plan to do special things often. Do not wait for special occasions or during times when there is tension or trouble or when you have done something that you need to apologize for. Making up or apologizing through romantic gestures is great, but if the person only feels loved when there is a crisis, other problems may occur. Please be mindful of that.

Most of all, enjoy your times together and always keep the romance alive and continue to make your partner feel special.

Conclusion

****

    This has been a book about readiness, the process of change, developing a positive, healthy self-esteem and finally finding and becoming involved in a wholesome, healthy, loving relationship.

    It has been about making choices and positive changes as you become ready to make them. It has also been about knowing when you are ready to make important changes in your life and recognizing when you are ready for change.

    I believe that change is necessary in order to grow and become ready to be in a positive, healthy relationship. However, I also believe that you can't do what you can't do, and that no amount of worrying, self-criticism, or willpower will help you make a change you're not ready to make.

    I believe that if there's a change you very much want to make and you've given it your best shot but you simply cannot make it; there's a good reason that you can't make it.

No matter who tells you that you are better off making the change, you will only change when you are ready. It's as simple as that. That's one of the things The Readiness Factor is all about, making the proper changes in your life when you are ready, willing and able.

When you are ready to commit to the right relationship, you will and when you are ready to make other changes in your life, you will. It's just that simple.

The most important thing to remember is that you will always need to work on becoming your best self. You will need to work on discovering who you are and what you can do to make your life even better. The necessary changes you feel you need to make in your life will be a little easier and the transitions will not be as hard if you move steadily in a positive direction.

Preparation is a process and takes time. Be easy with yourself and always move forward. Never look back.

When you have worked on becoming your best self and you want to bring a person into your life, I have listed several ways you may meet new people. Also, there are some dating tips and some suggestions on how to identify who's right and who's wrong.

Once you have found your "special someone", there are suggestions on how to keep love alive and how to continue to make your partner feel special.

Finally, this book has explained the in's and out's of relationships and how they change. It shows the reader how to make positive changes in relationships when he or she is ready and how to build a healthy, solid self-esteem.

The best of luck to you in your quest to prepare yourself for the ultimate relationship. Hopefully, this book has been and will continue to be a reference guide that will help you in your quest to develop a genuine love for yourself in preparation for loving another.

Godspeed!

Bibliography

****

Barone, Don & Sharon Faelten, <u>Lifespan-Plus</u> (Rodale Press, Inc. - 1990)

Bernfield, Lynne, <u>When you can, you will</u> (Lowell House Publishing - 1993)

Bombeck, Erma, <u>A Marriage Made in Heaven or Too Tired for an Affair</u>, (Harper Collins - 1993)

Branden, Dr. Nathaniel, <u>Raise your self-esteem,</u> (Bantam - 1987)

Brothers, Dr. Joyce, <u>Positive Plus</u>, (G.P. Putnam's Sons - 1994)

Carter, Steven & Julia Sokol, <u>Men who can't love,</u> (Berkeley Books - 1983)

Dyer, Dr. Wayne W., <u>You'll see it when you believe it,</u> (William Morrow - 1989)

Epstein, Alan, <u>How to have more love in your life,</u> (Penguin Books Ltd. - 1994)

Goldstein, Joan & Manuela Soares, <u>The Joy Within,</u> (Prentice Hall Press - 1972)

Morris, Lois & John Oldham, Personality Self Portrait, (Bantam Books - 1990)

Sills, Judith, Excess Baggage, (Penguin Books - 1993)

Smedes, Lewis B., Caring and Commitment, (Harper Paperbacks - 1988)

Solomon, Dr. Marion, Lean on me, (Simon and Schuster - 1994)

Viorst, Judith, Necessary Losses, (Simon and Schuster - 1986)

Wegscheider-Cruse, Sharon, Learning to love yourself, (Health Communications, Inc. - 1987)

Welwood, John, Journey of the Heart, (Harper Perennial - 1990)

Wolfe-Morgan, Lois, Build your own road, (Berkley Books - 1992)

ORDER FORM

You may order extra copies of <u>The Readiness Factor</u>.
Just fill out this form and return it to:

> MOTH, Inc.
> 3115 West 6th Street
> Suite C-100
> Lawrence, Kansas 66049
> (785)840-0518

You may also Fax this form to us at 785-840-9543

****

Please send _____ copies @ $12.95 each = $ _____
            plus shipping $ 2.95 1st book=$ _____
    each additional book $ 1.00   = $ _____
                      Total enclosed = $ _____

Please check one: Cash__ Check__ Money Order__
Visa____ Mastercard____

Card # _____ Exp. Date: _____

Signature: _____

Name: _____

Address: _____ Apt. # _____

City _____ State _____ Zip _____

Phone #(optional) _____

****

Dr. Thompson is sought after for seminars, conferences, lectures and workshops. She enjoys inspiring her audiences on the topics of relationships, esteem-building, and personal empowerment. For more information and seminar dates or to schedule a speaking engagement or conference, you may contact Dr. Thompson at the address and phone number above.

The Relationship Readiness Test

In order to determine whether you are ready for a relationship, please answer each question honestly with a **Yes** or **No**.

Esteem-Building
1. Do you say positive things to yourself and about yourself? Yes___No___
2. Do you feel you have the power within you to accomplish your specified and stated goals? Yes___No___
3. When you have a problem, do you face it, explore a possible solution and work toward that solution? Yes___No___
4. Are you able to accept your strengths as well as your challenges? Yes___No___
5. Do you freely compliment others? Yes___No___
6. Do you stand up for yourself and speak up for yourself when necessary? Yes___No___

Mental & Physical Health
7. Have you read at least 2 self-help books within the last 60 days? Yes___No___
8. Have you seen a therapist, joined a support group or had long, extensive relationship conversations with friends and/or family members? Yes___No___
9. Do you take at least one day every month to do something nice for yourself? Yes___No___
10. Do you exercise on a regular basis? Yes___No___
11. Do you eat healthy foods on a regular basis? Yes___No___
12. Do you acknowledge the positive parts of your body and work on the challenging parts of your body? Yes___No___

Spirituality
13. Do you have a solid spiritual base? Yes___No___

14. Have you attended a religious or spiritual ceremony within the last 2 months? Yes___No___
15. Do you participate in some type of spiritual ritual on a regular basis such as prayer, meditation, fasting, or chanting? Yes___No___
16. Does prayer and meditation help you to overcome personal problems? Yes___No___

Relationship Challenges

17. When you ended your last relationship, did you allow yourself to experience and work through the following stages: shock, denial, anger, depression, understanding and acceptance? Yes___No___
18. Have you truly forgiven your previous partners for any wrong doing? Yes___No___
19. Do you feel complete and whole even when there is no romantic relationship in your life? Yes___No___
20. Have you stopped picking the same type of person and the same type of relationship over and over? Yes___No___
21. When you are in a relationship do you maintain your own interests and friends? Yes___No___
22. When you meet someone that you are interested in having a relationship with, do you postpone sexual activities for at least a month? Yes___No___
23. When you are in a relationship, are you able to let the person know what your needs and wants are?

Independence

24. Will you go to a movie alone? Yes___No___
25. Will you go to a restaurant and eat alone? Yes___No___
26. Will you go to a book store alone? Yes___No___
27. Will you go to a coffee shop alone? Yes___No___
28. Will you attend a concert or other event alone? Yes___No___

29. Would you attend a singles dance, place a personal ad, join a singles club or do other activities to meet new people? Yes___No___

30. If you make a decision that you feel is good and a friend or family member tells you it is wrong, do you stick to what feels right to you? Yes___No___

Making changes

31. Have you identified specific things in your life that you need to change? Yes___No___
32. Are you open to making changes in your life that will have a positive effect on you? Yes___No___
33. Are you willing to work and do what it takes to meet new people? Yes___No___
34. Have you identified your basic fears and are you facing them and working on them? Yes___No___
35. Are you willing to make necessary changes in your life even though the process may be uncomfortable? Yes___No___

Scoring: Give yourself **3** points for each **Yes**. Add up your points.
Your Score: _____

Here's what your score means:

90 - 105 - You are ready to work toward finding a healthy, fulfilling relationship. However, go back and review your test. The questions you answered with a **No** are the questions you need to look at. These are the issues you need to work on When you have worked on these and can answer yes to them, Read Chapter 5 to find out ways and places to meet new people.

75 - 90 - You are almost there. You still need some time to work on some issues before going out there. Go back over your test. All questions that you answered with a **No** are the questions you need to look at. These are the issues you should work on. Take the next 60 days to work on these issues, then re-take the test. Read Chapters 1 - 4 to give yourself a boost.

Below 75 - There are a lot of issues you need to look at. Take an opportunity to work on yourself. Go back to the questions where you checked **No**, write these questions down and work on them one at a time. After you have worked on these for at least 60 days, you should re-take the test. Read the entire book for help and suggestions on how to work toward your preparation.

Notes: